POEMS OF HAMPSTEAD HEATH

AND REGENT'S PARK

By Dinah Livingstone:

Poetry Books:
Kindness (2007)
Presence (2003)
Time on Earth: Selected and New Poems (1999)
May Day (1997)
Second Sight (1993)
Keeping Heart (1989)
Saving Grace (1987)

Poetry Pamphlets:
St Pancras Wells (1991)
Something Understood (1985)
Glad Rags (1983)
Love in Time (1982)
Prepositions and Conjunctions (1977)
Ultrasound (1974)
Maranatha (1969)
Tohu Bohu (1968)
Beginning (1967)

Prose:
Poetic Tales (2010)
The Poetry of Earth (2000)
Poetry Handbook for Readers and Writers (1992)

Edited:
This Life on Earth (prose and poetry 2009)
Work: An Anthology (prose and poetry 1999)
Camden Voices Anthology 1978–1990 (poetry 1990)

Poems of Hampstead Heath and Regent's Park

Dinah Livingstone

Illustrations by Anne Mieke Lumsden

KATABASIS

First published on May Day 2012
by KATABASIS
10 St Martin's Close, London NW1 0HR
katabasis@katabasis.co.uk
www.katabasis.co.uk
Copyright © Dinah Livingstone 2012
Designed and typeset in-house mainly in 12 point Garamond
Printed in England by imprint**digital**.net
Front cover painting: *Hampstead Heath Ladies' Pond in Summer*
Back cover painting: *Regent's Park Heronry in Winter*
and Black and white drawings, all by Anne Mieke Lumsden

ISBN: 978-0-904872-46-0
Trade Distribution: Central Books
99 Wallis Road
London E9 5LN
(0845 458 9911)

British Library Cataloguing in Publication Data:
A catalogue record for this book is available
from the British Library.

ACKNOWLEDGMENTS

Some of these poems have appeared in *Acumen, Camden New Journal, Daily Express, London Magazine, Morning Star, Second Light* and in the collections *Saving Grace* (Rivelin Grapheme, London 1987) and *Time on Earth: Selected and New Poems* (Rockingham Press, Ware 1999).

NOTE

The poems were written over several decades. Some are new. Others, as well as appearing in the journals and books acknowledged above, have previously been published in Dinah Livingstone's Katabasis collections: *Keeping Heart* (1989), *Second Sight* (1993), *May Day* (1997), *Presence* (2003) and *Kindness* (2007).

CONTENTS

FOREWORD

Here's to the Public   11

POEMS OF HAMPSTEAD HEATH

At the Start	*January*	17
Kenwood in Winter	*February*	18
Longed-for Warmth	*March*	19
Piercing	*March*	20
That Old Fever	*April*	21
Millfield Lane	*April*	22
Counting Sparrows	*April*	23
May Be	*May*	24
Bird Sanctuary	*June*	25
Embodiment	*July*	27
Fellow Creatures	*July*	28
Do I Wake or Sleep?	*August*	31
Concert at Kenwood	*August*	32
Whispers	*September*	34
October 2001	*October*	35
Pressure of Life	*October*	37
Surviving	*November*	38
Shape	*December*	39

POEMS OF REGENT'S PARK

Allegro con Spirito	*January*	45
February Walk	*February*	46
Standing Pair	*March*	47
Colour	*April*	48
Habeas Corpus	*April*	50
Wallflowers	*April*	52
Birdman	*May*	53
Middlemost	*June*	56
Great Fish	*July*	59
Tea in the Park	*August*	60
The Acorn Man	*September*	61
Squirrel	*October*	63
November	*November*	64
This	*December*	65
Where I Belong	*December*	66

FOREWORD

Here's to the Public

No one pays to go into Regent's Park.
On this April afternoon
people enjoy the breezy sun
lighting the soft and the brilliant colours.
They loll on grass, stroll, chat
in English, Russian, Arabic –
London's 300 languages.
I'm on a bench by the heronry,
some birds on big untidy nests,
others in pterodactyl flight
bring twigs or tasty morsels.

Two young men in jeans,
shirtless – still pale –
and a bouncy young woman
walk by, laughing, teasing.
A father, minding his threesome,
calls to the smallest on a mini-trike
while the sister cycles in pink
and an older child outstrips them
on a cool scooter. The dad smiles at me,
pleased, self-deprecating.
A mum peeps round the sun hood
of her pushchair and says 'Boo!'
to her baby. Yes, they smile too.
Regent's Park is a public place
where people can breathe freely,
take their ease, interact
and quite often look happy.

No one pays to go on Hampstead Heath
where so many huge trees
are able to reach full stature,
oak, ash, beech, holly and hornbeam,
each shaped by its nature and history
so singularly beautiful,
yet together their quotient increases
offsetting, enhancing each other,
the whole transcending.

And look at all the different people,
some quite eccentric,
leading their lives, the public
owning the trees and open spaces,
while having their own conversations
or jogging or musing by themselves,
yet the pleasure of each adds to the atmosphere
an energy that is more than private,
heightened because joy is social.

I was invited to read some poems
to six-year-olds in a primary school.
They particularly liked a chorus
when they all grunted like a rude pig.
All sorts of children mixing together,
a teacher skilled at balancing
zest and order, a teaching assistant,
a decent amount of equipment,
paper and coloured pencils, a computer.
No one pays to go to that school,
so surely that is public rather than
those familiar to the Cabinet
where the entry price is pots of money.

Next door to the school is a public library
threatened with closure.
The children often use it,
there are plenty of books and DVDs.
The library is also for grown-up people.
Our children were born in a public hospital
or at home with a midwife on the national health.
At present no one pays
to go into our great museums.

That refusal to tax the rich,
that instinct to destroy everything free,
to slap a ticket machine by the Ladies' Pond,
to privatise, to exclude those without means,
is barbaric. A kindly civilised people
needs large common spaces open to all,
not gated egoistic hatred.
Here's to the public.

POEMS OF HAMPSTEAD HEATH

At the Start

On a sharp blue January noon
chasing days of depressing rain,
along the path past Highgate Ponds
dogs delight in the great puddles,
shuddering their muddy coats in glee.

'No, Rover!', 'No, Plato!'
gasp bespattered owners.
'Black doggy! Messy doggy!'
my grandson calls from his pushchair,
Then: 'Let me out! I want walk!'
Of course he lurches into soggy grass,
crowing: 'Squelch! Squelch! Squelch!'

Back on the tarmac he lumbers
with hunched shoulders: 'Rrrrr!
I'm a monster!' emerging from primal slime
into imagination and language,
shambling the long human road.

The buds on the trees are still shut fast
but today seem to promise
something will happen soon,
and from that high branch, voice
like a silver lancet, the robin singing
pierces the soul, the hope,
the pain, the beauty of it.

Kenwood in Winter

Cloud shapes pregnant-bellied
with rain or snow canter
over the twiggy trees. Blue patches
and the sun comes out, goes in.
Chattering boys, aged about ten,
dribble a ball across the soggy grass –
their eager yelps recede.

Under the ivy tunnel on a damp bench
two lovers, seeking seclusion, kiss.
Small children shrilly negotiate.
Good dogs trot while others gallop off.

Along the path pass families, couples, friends
engaging in little spats
or their peculiar conversations.
Some souls are solitary.

This February Sunday isn't warm,
but sitting out a while I see
how animate and inanimate
belong together to be themselves,
move with their own intensity
into one cool fusion, the living
even in winter so alive.

Longed-for Warmth

How welcome this March sun is
warming my winter body.

The wind has dropped. I lizard
on a wooden bench where lake laps,
water birds glide at ease
and quack a bit, background
noise detracting nothing from a
bonus, peaceful, lazing afternoon.

Only the quick nip
of a less simple neediness.

Piercing

Though patches of frosty shade
and puddles remain with jagged ice,
the naked willows' twigs shine tangerine,
supple and delicate they tang the blue.
Lake water whorls and ripples skimmed by gulls
and sunlight pours itself down muddy grass.
That screech is a green parakeet.

Briefly let off from winter drear,
strolling Londoners smile today
and lonely when I wandered out,
I feel a stab of joy,
sharp as the colours' edge,
the spurt of citrus fruit
and zest of that exotic squawk,
voice now becoming naturalised
among the parliament of indigenous fowls.

That Old Fever

All new this week, from naked bark
the soft shoots of the copper beech
are transparent sandy pink
beside the pale green willow.
The conker tree has filled
to a brilliant viridian ball,
its candles still in bud.

Busy quacking on the lake,
encouraged by kind sun
some birds are nesting now.
A gaggle of girls
dip toes in the water,
happily giggling and squealing.

With spring in my step
I wander elated,
though faintly lonely,
a bit out of it, grown
older after another winter.
This year will I be able
to catch that rhythm, sprout
anything new or hatch?

Millfield Lane

When Keats met Coleridge here in Millfield Lane
hard by the next pond up from the Ladies' Pond,
did the Highgate sage feel death in the hand
he clasped and pity the promising, younger man?
Another April now I see the trees return
they might have seen – oak, sycamore – and stand
ravished by the giants' delicate flowers, on ground
where they stood talking under this fresh green.
New-burst from sticky buds, horse-chestnut leaves
droop like unfledged birds until they spread.
Rabbits. Cowslips in a sunny ditch:
like the poets, these still share our lives
as fellow Londoners, interconnected,
re-affecting, making each meeting rich.

Counting Sparrows

Sparrows were two a penny
and hard to count as the hairs on your head.
I remember how they used to flock
cheekily for crumbs from café tables
outdoors in Regent's Park,
and what a racket they made
congregated in a bush
like the chapel of an enthusiastic sect –
cockney sparrows they were called,
such common birds.

Suddenly they went.
It was as if London's bird spirit,
its indigenous *nagual* or *chulel,*
had abandoned it.
Who would expect to mind so much
their sad small absence?

Last week I saw three in a tree
and yesterday in breezy April sun
I sat at Kenwood and watched
a couple pecking at the gravel.
'Glad to see you back,' I said,
'please increase again. Now I count you
because you are so few.'

Nagual and *chulel* are Mayan Indian words for a guardian animal spirit.

May Be

Dour, thorny, over-wintered
many ordinary days, once more
this sturdy, modest tree puts out
its curly, first green leaves,
then blossoms white with may,
flesh-scented unforgetting, wedding
hope of pleasant picnic weather,
ponds where we delight to bathe,
Londoners, here on our Heath,

with a sight – in answer
to so many mayday calls –
of a species feasting in kindness,
enjoying its best wine,
humanity together at last
in planetary celebration.
That which is not called amiss
the Good Old Cause
voices the maytree: belief flowers again.

I climb to the top of Parliament Hill
where kites are flying.
All London spread out below
shines in the beautiful morning.

Bird Sanctuary

Seals sunning themselves,
women all shapes and sizes sprawl
with bird's-foot trefoil, buttercups,
flowering grasses, wild geraniums
and self heal on the lower meadow
of the Ladies' Pond Enclosure.

Whish! goes a kingfisher,
its turquoise matching the dragonfly's,
bird akin to insect as woman is to seal.
On the next pond down, swans,
moorhens, ducks, coots
pursue their wild lives in peace.

It's called the Bird Sanctuary.
Switch off your mobile,
sisters under the skin,
twinned, one pond for ladies
and one is for the birds.

Embodiment

How beautiful each tree
full-bodied in July,
growing and itself
each year against the sky.

The purple copper beech –
no wine so rich and dark –
stands on the green hill
above the boating lake.

The body thickening
with sixty-seven years,
as does its consciousness
of what it sees and hears.

Connecting more to more,
memory and rhythm
body-history senses
aware their night must come.

My birthday and my grandson's
both fall in July –
what I love seen fresh
by his bright learning eye.

Fellow Creatures

To all my Fellow Creatures that shall view these ensuing lines —
GERRARD WINSTANLEY, LEADER OF THE DIGGERS

1

Dapple on velvet,
the young black cat with golden ripples
appropriates the ornate, high-backed
intricately carved oak chair,
stretches herself on its faded plush
mulberry-fool upholstery,
claims her legitimate throne
her sleeping seat.

In stillness after midnight
solitude's deep root flowers.
Outburst alleluia from the earth:
'Glory here, Diggers all!'
The burring chorus blazes
as humble humanity,
now marigold-haloed,
finally makes it home.

In darkness the moment of seeing,
hearing the not yet uttered.
Kneel on the silky mat
where two white harts stand
under a noble tree. I rest my head
against the chairback's padding.
A surprise bunch fills my arms:
the cat purrs, pulse of the universe.

2

These days every afternoon
heatwaves ripple over Hampstead Heath.
Laid back in the Ladies' Pond I gaze up
at blue through willow. I turn over
and with slow breast stroke continue.
A duck swims towards me speedy and neat.
I admire her elegant economy
and engage her kingcup-yellow eye.
Velvet water laps her as it laps me,
animals in one of our elements.
Two feet from my face
she veers off to the left.

Some swimmers have come here regularly
for years. Some leathery now
have seen nearly a century,
might have been suffragettes,
still battling on, benevolent pond spirits.
Solid as willow trunk in middle age,
sometimes I'm accompanied by nymphs,
my daughters – rosebay and water lily –
mermaid hair floats like weed.
Generations of useful bodies
in all their various modes.
Comfort of women.

On the walk back, a glimpse of men
doing flash acrobatics
from their pond's diving board.
Shock of difference. Sudden tension
is a swift physical reminder

that though death's the price of otherness,
life's pleasure is much sharper
and its teeming forms increase
only because Earth has two sexes.
An old man talks to a cock pheasant,
brings daily bread.
'He's all alone,' he says.

The copper beech glows on the hill.
A boy goes up the burnt grass path
carrying a scarlet kite.
Draggled dogs have a final paddle.
Londoners call them and their children home.
A giant poplar rustles
as the evening sunlight falls.

Do I Wake or Sleep?

Seed fluff floats from the willow herb,
wafts on the hot afternoon.
An orange butterfly flits
over the ripening thicket of bramble.
A rabbit nibbles and lollops on.

Interrupting the fertile quiet
a fat pigeon's wing feathers flap
as it alights on the birch.
It sounds like a belly flop
into the deep pond.

Minding its own business,
round the corner softly trots a fox,
unselfconscious till it sees me
half-dozing on a bench in shade.
Speakingly, it halts,
engages my eye and vanishes
as if it had never been.

Concert at Kenwood

Though the forecast
was torrential rain and gales,
it is a balmy evening. Calm and free
the picnic parties gather on rugs
behind the deckchairs.
Snug side by side
they patchwork all the grass,
quilting the concert field.
They unpack carrier bags and baskets,
corks pop. The expectant supper
is delicious out of doors.
Couples feed each other titbits,
birthdays are toasted in the setting sun.

After dark, in time with Nutcracker
emerald lasers pirouette and flit
among the leaves of the enormous trees,
beam brilliant active streams
across the lake from the lit concert bowl
and whorl on smoke as dancing holograms.

And light is rhythm, as it is our energy.
Tonight it refreshes jaded eyes,
liquidly coheres with hearing.
Light made the food for picnic stomachs.
Now as it satisfies with spectacle
it coalesces human groups,
attaches lovers, fastens friends
jointly enjoying its giant jig.

They become a celebration counterpane
spread over the hard ground
and I am touched when my delighted
grown-up daughter rubs my aching back.

Whispers

Drowsy in long, dry grass
on a warm blue day,
I lie beside this little copse
and listen to the rustling silver birch.
There's not much breeze but the downward
swaying leaves are never still,
and on the shiny, slender trunks
shadows wander constantly.

For days I've been crying inside
in a turmoil after a quarrel.
My thoughts dart about in a thicket,
struggling to articulate out of ugly,
necessary rage, something
not self-righteous yet genuine,
that might be communicable
in a mellower mode.

The sun caresses and comforts me
to a state where love and anger
are difficult to distinguish, just as
the restless motion of the weeping leaves
feels peaceful and glad,
my life, my energy not separate
from tree, grass, Earth and sky.

October 2001

War came. Bombs fell again.
Poor people try to flee,
clutching their ragged children,
towards winter without food.
They throng my eyes and mind
with helpless responsibility.
Fear of attack on London.
My dearest, beware the tube,
the fireball, seeping poison.

Meanwhile, on Hampstead Heath,
an autumn spurt of growth,
fresh brilliance in the grass
from spongy turf, my step more
elastic in the noble presence of trees,
each shape quintessentially distinct,
full-dressed in waving leaves
becoming radiant before they fall.
Life's sweetness aches the urgency of peace.

Pressure of Life

Arrangements, conflicts, contracts, creditors
crowd my busy head to bursting.
I thread through packed, thrusting punters,
a limp resident out for a bit of fruit
from Inverness Street Market,
who failed to remember it is Saturday
when Camden Lock is chock-a-block.
Back home I eat apples of exhaustion.

Later as I listen to leaves brushing
the azure-golden autumn weather
and watch a couple of soft white swans
glide slowly past on a Highgate pond,
I let myself be the rippling waters,
become the motion and the spirit that impels,
the same breath that earlier agitated to ugliness
the throng of jostling bargain-hunters
and me among them.

Surviving

Trees never stop growing
all their lives, you said.
But now in late November
hurricane-bereaved
of several airy branches,
whose strength was my joyful
breath and balanced me,
as well as suffering
my seasonal stripping of leaves,
I am dead tired,
slow, timid, holding off
the cold assault
with a must-be tough-rooted
skeleton belief.

Shape

I watch a graceful group of winter birch,
dappled brown and silver trunks,
whose twiggy filigree red tops
gently finger the sunny sky
pianissimo. Then two walkers pass
conversing in local cockney
about what's going on. I hear
their mouths form vowels,
typical labio-dental fricatives,
glottal stops, to make meaning, feeling
sound-shapes flowing like the silent
music of the outlined trees.

Beyond the static monolith,
over the oak's crown,
crows keep circling, settling,
each sharp black individual
convolving a moving pattern.
The rainbow's evanescent colours
interflow. Those beautiful young people
have grown from infant bodies
and are the same and not the same.
A loved face reappears, rhythm-reflected
in lapping water, dissolves, as sun goes in
and shapes shine only now and then.

As well as worse possibilities,
trying to set days, years, a life
in order, to become what is wanted,
has to confront the more humdrum

too tight shipshape, sheepish conformity,
slipshod *accidie*, that scupper the scope,
dull the sheen. That which
may have escaped or shun you,
nevertheless, gleams interstitially.

A grand narrative history
grows stale, needs re-imagining
with hope for the human race
that is the same and not the same.
Fundamentalism hates free growth,
as bound feet become misshapen,
trapped minds and spirits rigid,
murdered bodies shapeless lumps of meat.

Splendor formae, beauty so old and so new,
burns in the breast, and the instant caught
in a song sung, a still photo, a kiss,
belongs to Earth's musical living process,
with new poems that go on being written
out of the *tohu* and *bohu* of dreams
as long as language survives,
so that people talk to each other
and mean it, full-of-grace
birdflight, treescape, opening celandine
on which the sun has shone, all
shift, rest, swift, slow, breathing or
breathless, organic, daring and fallible.

POEMS OF REGENT'S PARK

Allegro con Spirito

By mid morning the ice has melted,
sun on the lake cheers swimming gulls,
ducks, black swans breakfasting
with their serpent necks.
High in twig nests on their island
some herons are at home.

Two willows stand by the water,
still trailing yellowed leaves
deep into winter, which dance
above the ripples, diaphanous
against each firmly rooted trunk's
historical dark form.

In the café a little girl,
hearing the sweet Mozart, can't resist
leaping from her seat
at the table with her family,
flapping her woolly pink poncho,
to jig about in time.

February Walk

Grey sunless sky and mud.
I heave my heavy body through the park.
Those uncouth cries are flocks of raucous youths
kicking footballs into dusk.
The energies displayed in it are fine.
Their cries in every language sound the same.

Now the light has nearly gone.
My mind shut tight like twigs,
the thin extremities of wintering trees,
it's hard to credit something's pulsing there
or lamb will ever struggle out of dark
to stand and bleat its individual poem.

Standing Pair

In the Spring sunshine,
two young ash trees
standing side by side,
quite close like lovers,
both in flower – one male
with thick brown clumps of seed
and very new sharp-shooting leaves,
one female, fanning out her fresh
green, heart-shaped, mini-petals
on slender stalks in an open posy
waving, dancing, beckoning,
her future fruits, the keys.
Both trees are utterly beautiful,
full of light
like you two on your wedding day.

Colour

For John Milton's 400th Birthday, 2008

Yes, cowslips are back,
a whole carolling bankful
draws me to the lake.
I drink in yellow
pealing from curly bells.
Out of wintriness
my walk quickens
and my spirits blaze.

Vermilion tulips
tremble fleshy and secret
in the stiff breeze
of a chilly April.
I shiver as the living scarlet
pervades my being here,
satisfies desire forgone,
forgotten by starved eyes.

Blue sky and hyacinths,
purple velvet pansies
and every kind of green,
as grass and leaf spring
fresh and sparkle in the sun
when it succeeds in shining
clear of active clouds.
Showers. Rainbow.

Dark, dark, dark,
without all hope of day.
The sun was dark to him,
Milton like his Samson blind,
heart-bleakening lack
of colour, light and joy,
his world cancelled. How come
his poetry never failed?

Habeas Corpus

When I am dead
were I admitted to heaven
I would not feel at home.
How I would miss the Spring.
I sit in an April garden
deep-blue-scented with hyacinths
amid yellow crown imperials.
Would I want a heavy gold crown
for a life achieved? I want this,
which changes every day,   '
one petal now ragged
where an insect has bitten in,
everything pressing, passing.

How I would miss the Summer
with higgledy-piggledy picnics
on the Heath, even when someone
gets lost, arrives late cross
and it threatens rain.

I prefer that to an angel choir
where I don't belong,
habeas corpus being
sine qua non
of a human song.

Untidy city with your muddle of people
living their lives, not knowing the future.
Earth with your beauty so old and so new,
that does not stay but slays me

again and again with each different recurrence,
kind and careless habitat
where love can flower (or not),
every body lives and dies
and the heart's desire tantalises.
I would be homesick in heaven
and hanker.

Wallflowers

A bed of red wallflowers
overpowers her, subtle
wafts on gusts of April.
Passionate in sunlight
the soft cruciferae reappear
after the hard dull length.

From dumb defeat she turns over
a new leaf to write.
With smile still secret
tongue, nipple and belly
wail for a new man,
recall skinsmell limbsflail.
She thinks she knows the one
but is biding her time for a while.

Birdman

The assistant birdman of Regent's Park
says he lives out in the sticks
in a village just past Watford.
In the morning he walks more than a mile
to the station to catch the 5.38 into Euston.
He wears paddling shorts showing hairy legs
and knobbly knees. Taken rather aback
by his Cockney-on-the-Costa physique,
a Hampstead couple with expensive binoculars
quiz him about his qualifications.

'When the job came up
my mate that works here
he knew I were a birder,
said why don't I go for it like
and well, I got it.'

He knows every bird in the park
to the feathers they add with the years.
A bleeper at his belt records sightings
of rare specimens elsewhere in England.
In the middle of the playing fields
he scans the sky and in sudden ecstasy
exclaims: 'Osprey! Osprey!'
With his whole body intending upward,
radiance streams from his face
like an angel.

Regent's Park is in the middle of a big city
and not near the river. These are just

some of the birds to be seen in it:
great crested grebe, Leache's petrel,
gannet, cormorant, shag, little egret,
grey heron, whooper swan, mute swan, spoonbill,
red-crested pochard, pintail, garganey,
mallard, shelduck, greylag goose,
widgeon, mandarin, gadwall, teal,
goldeneye, honey buzzard, kestrel, smew,
sparrowhawk, hen harrier, merlin, moorhen,
pheasant, grey partridge, corncrake, peregrine,
shoveler, oystercatcher, lapwing, coot,
whimbrel, woodpigeon, bar-tailed godwit,
golden plover, stone curlew, dunlin, snipe,
wryneck, herring gull, kittiwake, tern,
green woodpecker, woodlark, skylark, wren,
guillemot, turtle dove, barn owl, cuckoo,
sand martin, tawny pipit, ring ouzel, stonechat,
greater spotted woodpecker, kingfisher, swift,
sedge warbler, whitethroat, blackcap, chiffchaff,
carrion crow, yellowhammer, chaffinch, brambling,
song thrush, mistle thrush, fieldfare, firecrest,
nightingale, blackbird, dunnock, robin,
bullfinch, goldfinch, sparrow, siskin,
treecreeper, linnet, jackdaw, jay,
blue tit, great tit, red-breasted flycatcher,
long-tailed tit, nuthatch, great grey shrike,
greenshank, sandpiper, hobby, woodcock,
pied wagtail, yellow wagtail, magpie, rook.

Here beginneth the Parliament of Fowls:
The life so short the craft so long to learn,
th'assay so hard, so sharp the conquering...

And when this work all brought was to an ende,
to every fowl Nature gave his make,
by even accord and on their way they wende
and Lord, the blisse and joye that they make!

Middlemost

Within the outer circle
the inner
and there
what had been
the learning haven
became the unspeakable
sleek black nightmare
the appalling pounding
sudden squad car
uniformed men
having huge power
hustling one off alone
to abomination of desolation.

The outer circle
has a long lake with ducks on
parkland grass and trees
bandstand wafting tunes
then you cross to the inner.

The inner circle
flaunts the brilliant garden
crimson roses creamy
some memory-scented
stripy lawn with daisies
ornamental water
where willows dip
to kingcups and lilies
and a shallow curve of poplars
at whose feet fuchsias bow

shelters the central fountain
piled with mer-people.

Mirror of the soul
where an opulent grim hall
with howling chandeliers
houses the horror
heart of darkness
on the inner circle's rim

but within that
the garden glories
flagrant with red-hot pokers
subtle with mallow and cranesbill
tame squirrels to talk to
and oh, the oceans of roses
peace and grace abounding.
Quick in the middle
leaps the fountain
to sit still by
and feel love well.

Great Fish

Coming from beds of deep secret roses,
crimson velvet with swoony smell,
I stand by the lake bewitched.
The white, the black and the golden carp
glide silently under the water
at will like thoughts in the early morning
before they are organised
or memories still half submerged
in murky depths. They are so many.
Quick-slipping, their big bodies,
charged with graceful energy,
have the kick of an unborn child,
a person swimming into consciousness
with powerful emotions of the soul.

Tea in the Park

Thunder. Run for it?
Broken roses.
Acres of patient grass.
Weak tea for two
squashed under achieved roof.
Green rain on glass.
Eaves-dropped explainings.
Acceptance, friendship, grief.

Lulled peace trip
to a secret wildgrown garden.
Trees drip. Wet underfoot.
Hives have bees.
Among small rocks she shows
prolific dark columbines,
white cotton stitchwort,
buttercups, poppies, herb robert.

The Acorn Man

Today we made an acorn man
in Regent's Park.
We called him Midge.
He said: 'I am God.
I made the dark
and you and all these trees.
I am bored.
I want to go to Baker Street.
I cannot ride on the great cat.
I have enemies.
I want to go to Baker Street.
This is the iron bridge
hung with flowers and berries
which is my road.'

We went across.
'Put on my hat,' he cried.
'I am God coming to Baker Street!'
We put on his hat
and the youngest child
had her turn to hold him,
as we came
to that café by the station
where you can get cream buns
and all kinds of coffee.
Then she forgot
and dropped him.
He fell flat
in Baker Street.

Squirrel

'Them squirrels are a blinking nuisance,'
says my neighbour
when they dig up bulbs on her balcony.
I know another
who pops at them with an air gun.

But as I walk through Regent's Park
in the goldening afternoon,
how buoyantly they bounce along,
how delightful their agility at being
up a tree before anyone has twigged.

I crunch through fallen leaves
and see one with its bushy tail
curled against an oak, sitting upright
with an acorn in its paws
and what seems like a beady eye on winter.

Even though it's grey –
dismissed as not the correct kind –
I cannot help loving it,
and feeling glad it's active to survive.
Let it live.

I remember when he saw one
my grandson just learning to talk
sensed an immediate kinship
with his fellow creature
and called out in ecstasy: 'Cyril! Cyril!'

November

Their winter weakening of being
thins the leaves now burnished
in misty golden light
a little more each day.

From one tree all have left,
to show the body bare,
a standing Power,
attended at his feet
by minimal wild cyclamen.

Flutter, flit and tweet,
keen to survive the coming cold.
Each little rustle,
sudden or stray thought,
might be a bird
or a falling leaf.

This

The plane tree is a naked giant now,
its lacy and bobbled
delicate tracery revealed,
sharp against blue. Shape.
Its huge soul winters out.
I absorb its quiet in admiration.

How bodied the pigeon is
when it perches on bare branch.
Yesterday I saw one sat,
as if rehearsing the twelve days of Christmas,
but in a plum tree.

Its beady amber eye gleamed
on the deep gold fruits,
little magic lanterns still attached,
though all the leaves had gone.
The birdness of that bird:
its being made me glad.

Bird and tree are
and so are we.
Who needs God
when we share such selfhood?

Isn't God merely a codeword
meaning our human kind of self
not only is but may become
what we imagine in love and poetry?

Where I Belong

St John's Garden

*You have made us for yourself
and our hearts are restless
till they rest in you.*
— AUGUSTINE

Yes, I suffer that restlessness.
I always have, but no,
I will not address myself
to a god I don't believe.
But where can I go
for words of eternal life?

There is no eternity –
duration of that which does not change –
so where amid the changes and chances
of this fleeting world
set my heart? Can that be found?

Actually, Augustine, you were right
that seeking perfect circumstances,
the perfect man, the perfect place,
provides no solution.
Life in time flows on.

Fleeting, yes, but now and again. Today
by half past two on a mid-winter afternoon
the sun in this sodden garden
is beginning to set. Pale gold falls
on the rosemary's few blue flowers.

A chaffinch flits about the espaliered limes.
Where is peace? Not
in the waddling pigeon or bounding squirrel,
not even the clean silhouette
of the crow in the naked pear tree,
who will soon flap away.

Not in stasis. Not in possession
but belonging. Not
in that or this, but all of it
and me as part of it, sat on a wet seat,
haloed in earthlight,
which before teatime will be gone.